For Oscar and Ralph

The Author would like to thank BMW Plant Oxford;
Dr Charles Ambrose at Charles Trent Limited, Vehicle Dismantlers, Poole, UK;
and Mr Paul Rutherford, Chief Vehicle Advisor for their help and advice.

First published in Great Britain in 2007 by
Frances Lincoln Children's Books, 4 Torriano Mews,
Torriano Avenue, London NW5 2RZ

www.franceslincoln.com

British Library Cataloguing in Publication Data available on request

ISBN: 978-1-84507-635-1

The illustrations in this book are collages of torn papers.

Printed in Singapore

1 3 5 7 9 8 6 4 2

THE LIFE OF A CAR

Susan Steggall

F

FRANCES LINCOLN
CHILDREN'S BOOKS

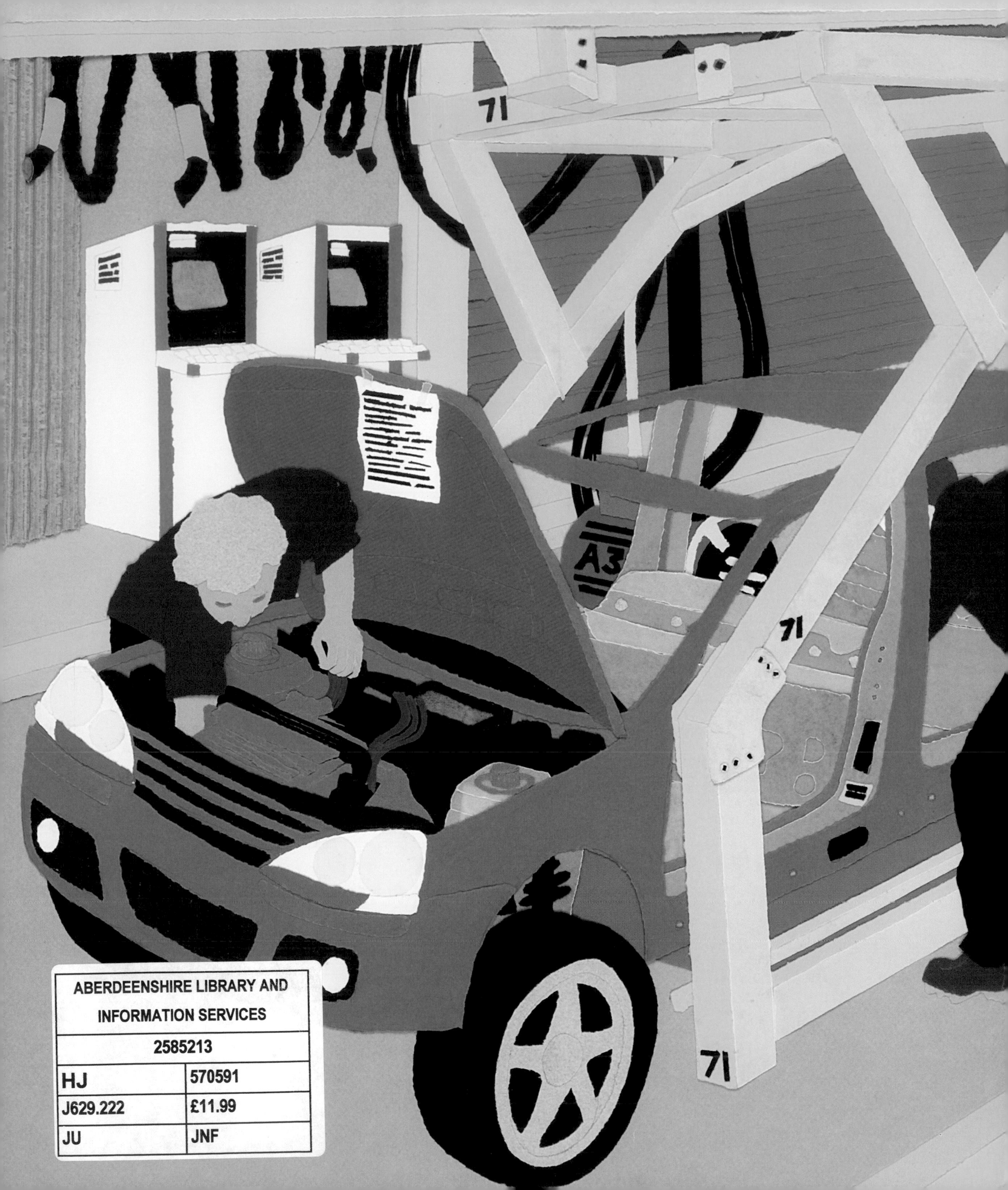
71
A3
71
71

Build the car,

deliver the car,

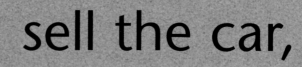

sell the car,

drive the car,

fill the car,

wash the car,

fix the car,

Tow the car,

strip the car,

crush the car…

to build a new car!